Little Guides to
Great Lives

FRIDA KAHLO

LAURENCE KING

Published by Laurence King Publishing Ltd
361–373 City Road
London EC1V 1LR
United Kingdom
Tel: +44 20 7841 6900
Email: enquiries@laurenceking.com
www.laurenceking.com

Reprinted 2019

Illustrations © 2018 Marianna Madriz
Series title designed by Anke Weckmann

A catalog record for this book is available
from the British Library

ISBN: 978-1-78627-300-0

Commissioning Editor: Chloë Pursey
Editor: Katherine Pitt
Design concept: Charlotte Bolton
Designer: The Urban Ant Ltd

Printed in China

Laurence King Publishing is committed to ethical
and sustainable production. We are proud
participants in The Book Chain Project®
bookchainproject.com

Little Guides to
Great Lives

FRIDA
KAHLO

Written by
Isabel Thomas

Illustrations by
Marianna Madriz

Laurence King Publishing

Frida Kahlo was one of Mexico's greatest artists. She lived during a time of huge change in Mexico and around the world, and was married to another famous Mexican artist called Diego Rivera.

But who was the real Frida Kahlo? This was the question she tried to answer through her paintings, including dozens of self-portraits—the artist's equivalent of a "selfie."

Frida wanted to show a "higher truth"—not just what she looked like, but her thoughts and feelings, and her connection to Mexico.

This is the story of how Frida became world-famous for painting the same thing over and over again—herself!

Frida was born in Coyoacán, Mexico, in 1907, to a Mexican mother and a German father.

Matilde Calderón y Gonzalez

Matilde was beautiful and elegant, but very strict, and was probably suffering from depression.

Magdalena Carmen Frieda Kahlo y Calderón

She grew up in the Casa Azul, a beautiful "Blue House" designed by her father.

Guillermo Kahlo
(Carl Wilhelm Kahlo)

Guillermo was a photographer. He immigrated to Mexico when he was 18.

Just call me Frida!

Frida had three sisters: Matilde, Adriana, and Cristina. Her father also had two daughters from his first marriage.

As Frida began her life, Mexico had a new beginning too. In 1910, the Mexican <u>Revolution</u> began as the people overthrew a <u>dictator</u> who had been in power for more than 30 years. It was a violent time and many people were killed.

Five-year-old Frida watched the fighting from the safety of her home.

"I remember watching a battle in the streets. The bullets just screeched past. I can still hear their extraordinary sound."

The spirit of the Mexican Revolution—the rebellion against power and the fight for fairness—appealed to Frida. She remembered hiding in a big wardrobe, secretly singing revolutionary songs.

These memories and feelings stayed with her for the rest of her life. She even changed her birth date to 1910 to match the year that the revolution began!

The fighting did not frighten Frida as much as her father's illness. Guillermo suffered from <u>epilepsy</u>, which Frida did not understand.

"He would often be walking along with his camera slung across his shoulder, holding my hand, and suddenly collapse. I got to know how to help him when these attacks occurred in the street."

When he was not ill, her father was warm and kind. He loved Frida's cheeky, rebellious nature.

Like all Mexican girls at the time, the sisters were taught to cook, sew, and look after the house. But not only that. Guillermo believed girls should get a good education just like boys, so he enrolled Frida and Cristina in a German school in Mexico City.

Sadly, tragedy struck Frida's life early, in 1914—when she was just six years old.

"It all began with a terrible pain in my right leg, which spread from the muscle down to my foot..."

Frida had caught <u>polio</u>, a disease that weakens muscles and can be deadly. It took nine months of rest in bed to recover. Even then, Frida was left with a weak and thin right leg and a right foot that stopped growing properly.

Suddenly, she felt different from everyone else, and lonely. At school, children gave her the nickname "Frida, pata de pelo!" [Peg-leg Frida].

Frida began to find comfort in her own imagination...

"On the window of my old room…
I used to breathe on one of the top panes.
And with my finger I would draw a "door"…

Through that "door" I could come out,
in my imagination, where my imaginary friend
always waited for me…And while she danced,
I told her my secret problems."

Guillermo came up with an exercise plan to help Frida become strong again.

roller skating

riding a bike

rowing

ball games

boxing

climbing trees

I didn't care that girls weren't "supposed" to take part in sports.

The exercise worked, and Frida's limp got better. Although one leg was still thinner and weaker, she emerged even more fearless than before.

Guillermo also taught Frida how to use his camera. Color photography had not been invented yet, so black-and-white pictures had to be colored by hand. Frida loved this work—it took all of her attention, and stopped her thinking about other things.

"I had a wonderful childhood, because although my father was ill, he was an extraordinary example to me of tenderness, hard work, and, most of all, in his understanding of all my problems."

At 14, brainy Frida passed an exam to get into Mexico's best school. Just 35 of the 2,000 students were girls, but Frida was not afraid of being different —in fact, she was starting to enjoy it. She often dressed in men's clothes, and shaved her hair short.

Frida quickly made a group of creative, clever friends who loved the same things she did, like books, jazz music, poetry, and <u>socialist politics</u>. The group was known as the Cachuchas, after their peaked caps.

Frida was happy and in love with life. She began dating one of the Cachuchas, called Alejandro.

Frida enjoyed learning about <u>anatomy</u>, <u>biology</u>, and <u>zoology</u>. She wanted to study medicine and become a doctor. But tragedy was about to interfere with her plans again.

The Accident, 17 September 1925

"I sat down at the side next to the handrail...
A moment or two later, the bus collided with a tram.

It injured everyone. Me most of all..."

Frida's entire body was broken.

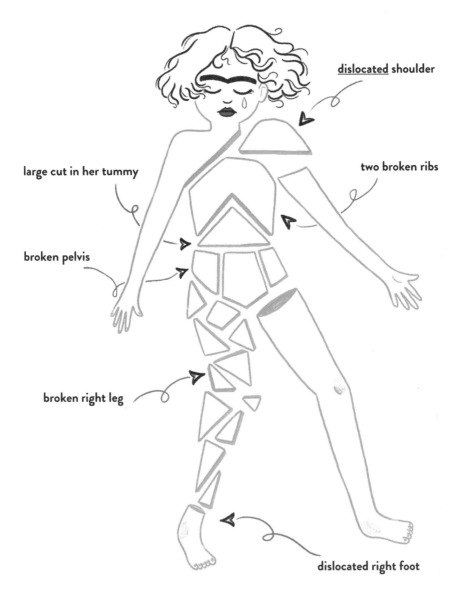

dislocated shoulder

large cut in her tummy

two broken ribs

broken pelvis

broken right leg

dislocated right foot

Several people had been killed by the accident,
and the doctors did not think Frida would make it.

Death danced around my bed at night

Everyone was amazed when Frida began to recover.
But her life would never be the same again.

Frida was stuck in bed for three months. Although pain, death, and sadness were often on her mind, her love of life and humor quickly bubbled to the surface.

Tuesday 13 October 1925

Dear Alejandro, you know better than anyone how sad I'm feeling in this pigsty of a hospital... Everyone says I mustn't despair, but no one knows what it means to me to spend three months in bed... Hey, at least la Pelona [Death] hasn't come for me!

Although Alejandro did not visit, Frida's other friends kept her company. She also read everything she could get her hands on—books about poetry, philosophy, politics, and art.

MANIFIESTO COMUNISTA

KARL MARX

Frida seemed to make a full recovery, but a year later she was back in hospital. Doctors discovered that three of her <u>vertebrae</u> were not in the right place. To correct the problem, she would have to rest for nine months, wearing plaster corsets to keep her spine still.

Although her dreams of being a doctor were over, Frida felt a tremendous energy inside. She wanted to do something with it.

Frida's father lent her paints, and her mother had a special <u>easel</u> made so that Frida could paint while lying down. Frida began to paint her friends and sisters and—with the help of a mirror fixed to the ceiling—herself.

When Frida was finally freed from her cast, she was 20 and ready to enjoy life again. She decided to focus on art. She had become obsessed with painting things just as she saw them.

Once again, Frida made a group of friends who shared her passions—Mexican artists who enjoyed discussing politics and wanted to see a fairer society.

Frida joined the Mexican <u>Communist</u> Party and wore their symbol pinned to her clothes.

Through her new artist friends, Frida met someone who would change her life as dramatically as the bus accident.

Diego Rivera
1886–1957
Famous Mexican painter

The new Mexican government were trying to bring the country together. They hired Diego to paint giant <u>murals</u> that celebrated Mexico's own folk art, culture, and traditions, instead of European history and art. The murals weren't just beautiful artworks, they were crammed with information.

Frida wasn't daunted by Diego's fame. She decided to find out what a serious artist thought of her paintings.

Diego remembered the moment forever, particularly Frida's striking eyebrows that met above her nose.

But most of all he was amazed by her paintings. He thought they were honest and real. Frida invited him to see more of her art, and they soon fell in love. Diego even painted Frida into one of his murals.

Frida got engaged to Diego, but her family were not happy. They thought of lots of reasons why Frida shouldn't marry him.

Diego is 21 years older than Frida.

Diego is so much bigger and heavier than Frida— it's like the marriage of an elephant and a dove!

Diego has already been married twice.

Our daughter is ill, and she will be ill all her life.

When they finally married, in 1929, only her father came to the wedding.

At first, Frida loved her new life. She began dressing in traditional Mexican costume every day, creating a different identity all of her own. And she painted more than ever. Diego inspired her. His praise helped her believe that she could be a professional artist too.

But things didn't go smoothly for long. The couple moved to San Francisco, in the USA, where Diego was hired to paint a mural. He loved being there, but Frida felt lonely. Diego was always at parties and meetings, while she found it hard to make friends.

I don't much like the gringos. They're boring and they all have faces like unbaked rolls.

In San Francisco, Frida faced tragedy again, when her first pregnancy ended. Her body had been damaged so much in the bus accident, doctors told her she would probably never be able to have a baby. Frida was heartbroken.

Frida was pleased when Diego had to return to Mexico for work. She loved being back among the wonderful sights, sounds, and smells.

They began to build a brilliant new house, but before long Diego returned to the USA—this time to New York. Frida didn't want to stay in Mexico alone, so she went with him.

Diego loved New York, but once again Frida was homesick and unhappy. She created an unflattering collage of the city, showing everything she hated about it...

"Americans live as if in an enormous chicken coop that is dirty and uncomfortable...

...the rich live in luxury right next to homelessness and poverty...

...people pretend to be something they are not...

...the only color is my Mexican costumes..."

Diego's next mural was in Detroit—a city of factories and machines. It was a much poorer area of the USA, but Frida and Diego found it more welcoming than New York.

However, while Diego painted one of his greatest masterpieces, Frida was recovering from losing another baby.

This time she painted like never before. Her self-portraits showed the terrible thoughts and images swirling around in her head. She was not afraid to paint her heartbreak and pain.

Even Diego was astonished. He said, "No woman had ever put as much poetic sorrow on canvas as Frida."

At last, in 1933, Frida and Diego moved back to
Mexico and into their new home. It was more like a
piece of art than a house, with two separate cubes
linked by a bridge.

Frida lived in the small cube. She filled it with exotic pets, including cheeky spider monkeys, cute baby deer, birds, and tiny, hairless Xoloitzcuintli dogs.

But her happiness did not last for long. In 1934, while Frida was recovering from an operation, she discovered that Diego was in a relationship with her younger sister Cristina.

Frida moved out of their home, and into a small flat in Mexico City. She didn't try to hide her heartbreak. Instead she painted it.

She even began a new relationship herself, with a talented sculptor. But deep down she still loved Diego...

...Even if we have to put up
with endless outbursts from
one another, door banging,
furious insults, and phone calls
from the other side of the world,
we will always love each other.

Frida's paintings became even more powerful, as she found new ways to show her worries and emotions.

She gave many of her self-portraits a plain, empty background, to show how lonely she felt.

Eventually, Frida returned to Diego, who continued to encourage her painting. In 1938, Frida held her first solo exhibition, in New York's Levy Gallery.

It was a great success—critics loved it, and she was asked to create more paintings. Frida was making money from her art, and becoming a star!

Next, Frida was invited to show her paintings in Paris, where her work made quite an impact. The Louvre, the world's largest and most famous museum, bought one of Frida's paintings!

Even Picasso, one of Europe's most famous artists, gave Frida a pair of earrings to show his respect.

Some people saw Frida's paintings as <u>Surrealist</u>. This type of art tried to show what was really going on inside the mind, and was often more like dreams than real life. But Frida disagreed.

I never paint dreams. I paint my own reality.

She was trying to paint life as she experienced it. She painted self-portraits because she was the person she knew best.

By 1939, the world was in turmoil, and Frida's life was in turmoil too.

She returned from Paris to find that Diego and Cristina were together again. In November 1939, as the Second World War began, Frida and Diego divorced.

Sometimes Frida felt despair.

Now I feel so rotten and lonely, that it seems to me that nobody in the world has to suffer the way I do...

At other times, she was full of hope for the future. She painted herself over and over again, finding different ways to show her feelings.

In *The Two Fridas*, Frida is holding hands with herself. She shows herself before and after Diego loved her, and how she uses her inner strength to heal her wounds, just as her imaginary friend had helped her cope as a child.

In *Self-portrait with Cropped Hair*, Frida has cut off her long hair and wears a man's suit. She shows that she is independent, and ready for the freedom of a new life.

In 1940, Frida visited San Francisco, where she saw Diego again. He asked her to remarry him, and she said yes, but only if she could remain independent.

We will live separately. I will make my own money by selling my paintings.

I was so happy that I agreed to everything.

Frida was a successful artist now, and life was calmer, but her health was getting worse as her spine became weaker and weaker. She was forced to spend most of her time at home, so she filled her house with trees and flowers, beautiful Mexican crafts, and pets.

Many of Frida's pets appeared in her self-portraits, as did the plants and landscapes of Mexico.

As Frida's fame grew, she was invited to be a professor of painting at the Mexican School of Painting and Sculpture.

Unlike most teachers, Frida didn't ask her students to copy famous paintings. Instead, she showed them real Mexican life.

She took them on trips to her beautiful garden and colorful markets, to poverty-stricken <u>shantytowns</u>, and interesting historical sites. She even arranged for her students to paint their own mural in the street.

When Frida became too ill to teach at the university, her students came to her house for lessons instead.

Frida was only 37 now, but her back was so weak that she could barely sit or stand. She could often do nothing but lie in bed, wearing a steel corset. Frida began keeping a diary filled with sketches, collage, and writing. As in her paintings, she tried to express her deepest thoughts and feelings, even if they didn't seem to make sense.

In 1946, the Mexican Ministry of Education awarded Frida a prize for one of her paintings. Although Frida was often in a lot of pain, she came to the prize ceremony, and continued to paint.

In *Tree of Hope, Stand Firm* she painted two different versions of herself: Frida on the outside, lying in a hospital bed at the edge of a bottomless pit...

...and Frida on the inside, dressed in beautiful clothes, sitting up and holding a banner that says "Tree of Hope Stand Firm."

The painting shows that even in the most difficult times, she could find courage inside.

ÁRBOL DE LA ESPERANZA MANTENTE FIRME.

I never lost my spirit. I always spent my time painting.

In the last years of her life, Frida's paintings show how she often thought about death. But she still managed to find hope and strength.

Friday 30 January 1953

In spite of my long illness, I feel tremendous joy in BEING ALIVE.

In 1953, Frida held her first solo exhibition in Mexico. She was determined not to miss out, arriving by ambulance and hosting the show from a bed at the center of the gallery.

By 1954, Frida's health was worse than ever. But she continued to fight for a fairer, more peaceful world, holding a banner with a dove of peace at a political demonstration. Frida died eleven days later, on 13 July 1954.

Since her death, Frida has become even more famous. Today her paintings sell for millions, and copies hang in homes in Mexico and all around the world. Books and films celebrate her life.

Frida made small paintings with big themes. They show us that sadness, pain, and loss are a normal part of life. But they also show how the courage, hope, and passion we have inside can help us to cope, whatever life throws at us.

One of Frida's last paintings was of colorful watermelons, with her final message to the world— "Live life."

TIMELINE

1907
Magdalena Carmen Frieda Kahlo y Calderón is born in Coyoacán, Mexico, on 6 July. She is known as "Frida."

1910
The Mexican Revolution begins. It has such an impact on young Frida that she later claims 1910 as the year of her birth.

1914
Frida catches polio and has to spend the next nine months in bed to recover.

1927
Finally free from her cast, Frida joins the Mexican Communist Party.

1928
Frida meets the famous Mexican painter Diego Rivera. They marry the following year.

1930
The newlyweds move to San Francisco. Frida is unhappy and homesick.

1933
Frida and Diego finally return to Mexico and move into their new home.

1938
Frida holds her first solo exhibition, in New York's Levy Gallery, which is a great success!

1939
Frida paints *The Two Fridas*, one of her most well-known works. Frida and Diego divorce.

1946
The Mexican Ministry of Education awards Frida a prize for *Moses*. She paints *Tree of Hope, Stand Firm*.

1953
Frida holds her first solo exhibition in Mexico. She hosts the show from a bed at the center of the gallery.

1954
Frida dies on 13 July, aged just 47.

1922
Frida enrols in the National Preparatory School, where she enjoys studying anatomy, biology, and zoology.

1925
On 17 September, Frida is in a bus accident in Mexico City. She is badly injured and, once again, has to spend months in bed. She seems to make a full recovery...

1926
...but a year later, the doctors discover problems with her spine, and she is bedbound for another nine months. Frida begins to paint to pass the time, creating her first self-portrait.

1931
The couple return to Mexico for five months and begin work on a new house, though they soon return to the USA—this time to New York. Frida begins *My Dress Hangs There*, though she does not finish it until 1933.

1932
Frida and Diego move to Detroit.

1940
After her divorce, Frida paints *Self-portrait with Cropped Hair*. She remarries Diego that same year, on the condition that she remains totally independent.

1943
Frida paints *Self-portrait with Monkeys* and becomes a professor of painting at the Mexican School of Painting and Sculpture.

1944
With her health getting worse, Frida is often forced to lie in bed, wearing a steel corset. She paints *The Broken Column* to show her pain.

Today
Frida Kahlo is remembered for her incredible self-portraits, colorful dress sense, and her courage in the face of adversity.

Frida Kahlo

GLOSSARY

anatomy – the study of the bodies of humans, animals, and other living organisms.

biology – the study of all living things on earth, including how and why they came to be and what factors continue to influence their development.

communism – a political theory based on the belief that all wealth should be shared and everyone should be treated equally.

communist – a person who believes in communism. Communists typically belong to a communist party.

dictator – a political leader who has complete control over a country, and often keeps control by force.

dislocate – to force a bone out of its normal position.

easel – a frame designed to support an artist's work while he or she is working on it.

epilepsy – a brain disease that causes sudden periods of uncontrollable, violent shaking, known as seizures.

gringo – a term used in Spanish-speaking countries, which refers to a foreigner, usually an American.

mural – a large artwork, usually a painting, made directly on a wall.

polio – a serious disease that weakens the muscles. There is no cure for polio, but it can be prevented by an injection.

revolution – an aggressive overthrow of a leader or government by a group of people who believe that someone else should be in power. Revolutions often bring about a period of violence and unrest.

shantytown – an area in a city or town where people live in poorly made houses.

socialist politics (socialism) – a social theory based on the idea that all land and businesses should be owned by the community as a whole, rather than individuals.

Surrealism – a twentieth-century artistic movement that explored dreams and their power to reveal our innermost thoughts and desires.

vertebrae – a group of 33 small bones that are stacked on top of one another to form the spine. The vertebrae protect the spinal cord and support the weight of the body.

zoology – the study of animals, including their structure, behavior, and habitats.

TRANSLATIONS

p53: "Yo soy la Desintegración" means "I am falling apart."
p57: "Despierta Corazón Dormido" means "Awake, Sleeping Heart."

INDEX

CREDITS

Photograph on page 61 courtesy of Granger Historical Picture Archive / Alamy Stock Photo

Frida's own words are quoted from *Frida Kahlo: 'I Paint my Reality'* by Christina Burrus (Thames & Hudson, London, 2008) and *The Diary of Frida Kahlo: An Intimate Self-Portrait* by Carlos Fuentes & Sarah M. Lowe (Bloomsbury, London, 1995)